The Essence of My Soul

A collection of poems
By
L'vette Sonai

Daisy Scout Publishing

Nashville ~ Los Angeles

No part of this book may be used or reproduced in any manner whatsoever without written permission except in the case of brief quotations embodied in critical articles and reviews.

The Essence of My Soul
Copyright 2016 L'vette Sonai
ISBN - 13: 978-0692691830

Daisy Scout Publishing
Nashville ~ Los Angeles

Also available are novels from author L'vette Sonai:
The Mulholland Diaries
The Hollywood Girl (a Mulholland Diaries Novel)

Interior Author photo: Lori Thomas

contact@lvettesonai.com
www.lvettesonai.com

"There comes a point when you've got to get out of your own way."
~ Unknown

One of the most difficult things for someone to do is reveal their heart and soul to the world. My personal experiences of joy, love, heartbreak and pain have taught me to rely upon myself; looking to my inner strengths to be happy. I have forgiven myself for not being perfect. I have learned to love myself enough to let God guide my path to the peaceful place of where I am in my life today. The following pieces stem from my most private and personal feelings through the past twenty years. Like a bleeding heart. They have been compiled in the order that they were written. Between these lines is where you will find my story. It has been a road of trials and mistakes, growth, depression and heartbreak and finally true love and happiness. I hope you enjoy this revealing journey as much as I have.

These poems are dedicated to everyone who has ever felt alone in their internal battles. Be your own best friend and love yourself. Never give up. You *will* survive and come out successfully.

Much Love,

L'vette xoxo

The Essence of My Soul

<u>90's</u>

A Naked Ocean

For My Sisters

The Strongest Bond

<u>2000's</u>

Valuable Journey

Black Male

Degree of Womanhood

Keep Focused on the Mountain

Of Beauty and Love

The Best of Me

The Power of Beauty

Metaphoric Dreams

Thank You for My Broken Heart

The Reason

Toxic Night

Me, My Father Forgave

Untitled

Blessed Revelation

You Are

<u>Late 2000's</u>

Familiar Stranger

Miss Opportunity

What Lies Beneath

I Feel

Zero Gravity

Of a Child

She Speaks

Wanderlust of My Mind

Don't Call Me Barstow (from The Hollywood Girl)

The Poet Tree

A Naked Ocean

I am of the wind tossed sea
Naked and distorted
My thoughts are ocean waves,
Anxious and defensive
I am like a naked ocean
As blatant as the moon on a clear and
dark night
My soul lies bare
and is exposed outright
My emotional sands are hidden
beneath the sea
I can only hope you'll come searching
through the depths of me
Like a tide seeking solace
on restful shores
I look to your arms
You're my serenity source
The winds of nature guide me
to your heart
Like two rivers meeting at an ocean
Where infinity starts...

For My Sisters

This is a letter for my sisters
Sisters before me
and those who follow
When we face difficult times and
sometimes affliction
Keep your heads up
In the strong black woman tradition
Like women who were spat on
and put down
Against their will men did lay
The women who endured pain deeper
than ours today
The women who taught their
daughters when there were no books
The women who taught us to gain
strength from the most piercing looks
Keep your heads up, my sisters
For I know of your pain
What does not kill you
brings your strength again
Beautiful sisters, most of all
Trust in Jah above
For there is nothing we could fail at
with his strength and love

Sisters before me
and those who follow
May we all grow together
hand and hand
For a more peaceful tomorrow

The Strongest Bond

I had searched so long
for someone to love
I felt I had to be in love
and why?
Because 'they' were in love
Being in love means this
and it means that
I fooled myself for so many years
Gone through so many tears
The love I found was lacking
compassion, morality, sincerity,
loyalty and honesty
The traits of which are like that of a
friend
I've discovered within my heart
That a friend would never try to hurt
me or put me down
A friend connects with my soul
and cherishes it
This is how my soul has connected
with yours
A friend is one you can count on, for
all of your life
Someone who is there at life's highest
and lowest moments

Their main focus is looking out for
your heart
To surround myself with positivity and
not just a good time
That's the love of true friends
The kind I hope to be yours and mine

Valuable Journey

Stepping off the porch of my haven
called Home
I stared out into an open field
A field of dreams
One of nightmares, of challenges
and schemes
I took a deep breath
to prepare myself
for what may lie ahead
Fear began almost immediately
With each step taken, I began to dread
Leaving the protective walls of home
There's something out there that
I had to find
Someone I had to meet
Searching through the weeds
I tried to find it
With little success
I continued my journey
As darkness surrounded me
I became tense
At some moments breathless
I felt weak from the anxiety of it all
Trying not to fall
I turned around to look at the home

I had left
Yet, I knew I must continue on
It will be there when I need
to gain strength
So I kept on pressing on
Reaching down into the care pack
Mother gave me
I drank of the wisdom
she put away for me
I ate of the fruits of the spirit
I was educated with
I gained strength and energy
to keep pressing on
I know I can find it,
I encouraged myself
Searching around the wooded field
Although about to give up
I finally found what I set out to
capture
Myself.
My own sense of being
My inner courage which I had lost
long ago
I was alone there physically
But, with the care given me and the
map of spiritual vision
I found the power I had built up

To survive in this wooded dark world

Black Male

All my life I have tried to understand
The complexity of the black man

Full of strength and passion
You stand as a leader
Someone I've looked to all of my life
My protector, my guide
Will you listen if I confide?
My sisters often tell me, go try
something new
Finding a good black man is becoming
far and very few
Examples of past lovers
put my loyalty to the test
But, to abandon the brothers to pursue
all the rest...?

All of my life I've tried to understand
The complexity of the black man
I think my heart has begun
to figure this out
What this love thing is all about

Fellow sisters, Nubian queens
This is what loving your man means

Open arms or a soft embrace
Fuels strength to him
For whatever he may face
Try to love him for whom he is
Hold a scolding tongue
Perfect never will he be
But his heart will surely be won

Degree of Womanhood

Sisters, can you hear me?
Can you feel where I'm coming from?
I feel a need to reach out to you
A need to extend my knowledge
And teach from my experiences of life
Though somewhat naïve I may be
I have a degree in womanhood
Which I've earned by way of love,
pain, sorry and loss
Yes, that's what taught me
Any girl can put a face on
But, only a woman
will rise up to the occasion
and stay strong
Sisters, can you hear me?
Can you feel where I'm coming from?
A lover lost, is a credit earned
No longer sitting in that corner
Crying over being burned
Keep remembering this,
as every sister should
Being a survivor is in our blood
Never accept what is less
Than what Grandma said is best
She held her head up

When degradation was her test
To be queens, that's our inheritance
So please, let us never forget
Take a young sister by the hand
Lead by gracious example
Towards being her best

Keep Focused on the Mountain

To continue on in this difficult world
Can be a test of one's faith
At every corner, every turn
Disappointment is what we face
Yet, I keep focused on the Mountain
I keep my eyes on the promised future
When all will be brothers and sisters
Living in peace
Crystal streams and sparkling rivers
Replace rubble and broken streets
The time is nearing for the promised
Paradise
When every day will have blue skies
A perfect life is what we can gain
If we keep our eyes on the prize
A time when children and wildlife play
together on grassy plains
An abundance of joy is to be gained
To recognize God as Almighty
and upkeep his laws
Of us is all that is asked
though so often we forget
Even take His love for granted
Neither of us does He wish to pass

When pressures of life begin to
overwhelm
Gather at the foot of the Mountain for
strength
From God's spiritual realm

Of Beauty and Love

I've always been told that I've been
blessed with beauty
To that there is some truth
For being beautiful means
to be full of beauty

I work hard to share my love
Love of God, love of freedom
That which he has given us
is true beauty
The things which makes life so
meaningful

There are so many hard times
more of which are to come
Having faith is what holds my head up
Extends encouragement
So that my fellowman may be won
from discouragement

Helping a struggling child pronounce
a fierce word
Brings joy to the heart
A place of unselfishness
Is where true beauty starts

Extending a hand to a stranger
When their heart is compromised
Faced with imminent danger
Trying to ease the fear in their eyes

Now is a time for us to recognize
That love stems deeper
than romance and desire
It starts with compassion
For our mankind
And, is instilled in us
From One much higher

Peace and Love 4 one another

The Best of Me

Do you feel me?
Really want me
Do you really want to know me?
Or just try to own me

Many men have said they loved me
Feel so good around me
The only truth is
They were better off
for having known me

Be for me, not against me
Because my adoration for you
Is what motivates me
I'm telling you
You bring out the best in me
You make my heart sing
and, my soul flow freely

This is why I ask you
Do you really feel me?
Really want me
Do you really want to know me?

I just want to be real for you

Just be there for me
For you will see the very best of me
So, let your love set you free

To be loved unconditionally

The Power of Beauty

My image stares back at me
Through the looking glass
She follows me
Pulls against me
Like a nemesis
Trying to destroy me
I become dependent
Her overwhelming thoughts
Direct my decisions
I become fearful
Yet, can't live without her

My image stares back at me
Through the looking glass

Like an enemy
Laughing in my face
Her power overtakes me
Beauty has her way
With my unnerved soul
Bringing me often to tears
Anxious with constant fears
An internal battle
Between her and me
I am defenseless

So powerful is she
Trying to corrupt
My pure and descent being
She has had me in her grips
Since I was a preteen
I have learned to square off
Look her in the eyes
Realizing the power which is stronger
In my heart is where it lies

Metaphoric Dreams

Hidden passions are coming alive
Like a flickering flame inside of me
As if to the alarm of pure ecstasy
I'm wanting to experience
Life's strongest emotion
Wanting it to take hold of me
Like a tide to the ocean
Recalling the moments
From when we first met
I knew you were my dream lover
The one I thought I would never get
I'm lying here near breathless
Imagining you caressing me
The love scene is set
To be played out
By you and me
Your strong hands
Begin to play my strings
Like a soloist in a symphony
Sensually stroking the keys to my soul
Releasing accolades within me
Tears of joy trickle from my eyes
Like soothing raindrops
Pouring down from heaven's skies
I am caught so deep

In my passionate dream
I am almost paralyzed
Startled as I awaken myself
Only to discover
Thoughts of the beauty of this man
Is like a prelude of my masculine lover

Thank You For My Broken Heart

I remember wanting you so
By any means necessary
The memory of being with you
Now seems a bit scary
So innocent and naïve
I thought chasing was the only way
I thought I had to do things
To encourage you to stay
It's funny how the tables can turn
No longer for you do I yearn
My phone constantly rang
The sound of pitiful words
and weak begging as it seems
I no longer want you by my side
Must be difficult
Understanding goodbye
I can recall those words from
when you spoke them to me
Fly away little boy
You are too pitiful to see
I have been emancipated
From the chains around my heart
I should have known
You were a liar from the start
In some ways you did me a favor

Gave me time to discover a new flavor
A real man does exist
for a woman like me
A lesson never would I have learned
Had you not hurt me and set me free

So, one last thing before we depart
I want to thank you
For my broken heart

My false love rest in peace

The Reason

Why should I care?

Why should I care about this world
and what's going on in it?
Mr. TV-Man says there is a war
going on
and this country is going to win it

Why should I care about my neighbor
and the fact that he lost his home in a
fire?
His wife of forty years consumed by
the blazing tragedy

Why should I care that a little boy
running happily across the street
was just run over by a drunken driver?
Or, that kids playing in the park must
dodge stray bullets
instead of a kickball

Why should I care that Brothaman
beat his woman to her dying breath?
I didn't know them

It sure was sad though, about the
unborn baby's death

Why should I care?
Why do you care?

I tell you, the next time I try to help
someone open up their heart,
Only for them to ask,
'why should I care?'
I have to tell them
Love is the reason
The only one that doesn't fail

Never was it God's intention
For us to suffer such pain and strife
He gave up his only Son
To save my life

All of this selfishness
and venomous hate
Finds us enslaved to a desperate state
Now is the time
To open up our hearts and minds

God cares.
Who are we not to?

Toxic Night

The memories of drunkenness
Creep into my numbed senses
I walk amongst sweat and fear
How did I get here?
In the heat of night

Wandering in my dream state of mind
I chance upon my subconscious faith
The antidote for my wasteful past

As my feet quicken their pace
I envision my mother's face
The one who always pulled me
From that darkened place
of turmoil and hate
The reason I'm still here

If ever I failed to believe
That love can save
This night is not that time
For as my heart feels the piercing
needle of pain
She nurses me and feeds me with love

Withdrawal from self-destruction
Is a monster and it is hard to let go
But, the newfound love for me
Thoughts of turning around
To a positive style of life
Gives me the okay to do so

I have awaken from the nightmare

Me, My Father Forgave

Born a babe of innocence
I was the apple of his eye
My Father's protective arms cradled me
A perfect relationship was nigh

Experiencing what life had to offer
I often seemed lost and confused
Naïve I was to the world
Left feeling oh, so used

Suffering the pressure
To go along with the crowd
I fell upon ill times
My conscious was like a sharp sword
Piercing my Bible trained mind

I often bled sorrowful tears
Yearned for Father to hear me
I called his name out loud at night
Hoping he would break me free

An open confessional of my secret life
Rid my aching heart of the pain and strife
I received my father's love
Along with loving care

While on my sleeve I wore sorrow and shame
Father said for my downed heart
he would be there

It's been a while since my shameful state
and all it weighed upon my soul
The relationship between Father and me
Is now more precious than pure gold
The love of my dear Father
Never should we take for granted
For my shame, once my heaviest burden
With His loving mercy, has been recanted.

Un*ti*tled

Sitting and staring
out at this dark night
I'm trying to understand
our relationship's plight

Never have I longed
for someone to know
That my admiration for them
Away never will it go

There is no denying
I want you to be mine
But to rush you along
only reverses precious time

My heart is in this for the haul
and whatever that may bring
I'm hoping beyond all hope
That this isn't just a thing

Realizing that sometimes
People want to tag on labels
Bringing a certain timeline
Pressure to the table

There is one thing only
I need you to realize
There has never been a man
Who with kindness and words
Brought real tears to my eyes

I will forever adore you

Blessed Revelation

As I think back when
I was only but a girl
There were glittering dreams
Of having an abundance
of love surrounding my world
I would envision my dream lover
With strong arms protecting me
Like a knight's shield
In my fantasy
For him to love me forever
seemed so real
Awaking to the dimmed reality
Of my challenging womanhood
I realized that not all admirers
were in it to seek out my good
There was much heartbreak
and many burning tears
Followed by dreadful fears
That I would never find
The man from my dreams
Of earlier years
I ceased chasing romance
To focus on my self-worth
Discovering love and where it starts
For me was like a rebirth

Once I began to understand it all
By being responsible
For my own happiness
Is when my true love came along
My fears of falling in love
Have faded in the wind
A revealing truth
From words years ago
Told me by a friend
You search for love
Seeking out passion
And when the love of your life appears
He will be better than you imagined

You Are

You are my moon that glows
And a star that shines
You are my sun which beams brightly
Of which I want no shade

I breathe of you

You are as fuel to my fire
My yearning desire
To love

I adore you

You are what a girl's dreams are
A beautiful man
A strong brother
A potential soul mate
A lifelong lover

And for me
You have no knowledge
Of what you are
No thought of how deeply
Your presence touches my soul

One day
Some day
You will know me
You will know us
You'll realize who you are

To me

Familiar Stranger

Woke up this morning
Gliding towards the door
This place is familiar
Though, never seen before

Caught up in a windstorm
Of emotional turmoil
Wondering how I got here
What it's pulling towards

The vision is scary
One that makes me weary
Remembering words that tear apart
The solace of my soul

I can't break away
Looking for another way
This fear in me is real
Though it's clearly a fake

Caught up in a windstorm
Of emotional turmoil
Wondering how I got here
What it's pulling towards

My world is crashing fast
Just how long this will last
I am wearing down
To a place I've known before

Never want to go back there
Never shall I return
To the place that broke me
See, I still wear the burns

It's over, it's wrapping
Awaken to a dream – that is reality

Miss Opportunity

Looking through a window of
opportunity
It all seems to surpass me
As I dream
Always a dreamer
Of living life as I want
Not being enslaved
to other people's wants
Other people's taunts
Not a slave to the games
that people play
Instead living for a better today

I'm not focused on tomorrow
For it may never come
But I need a resolution
Of getting what I want

There may never be chances like these
Doing just what I please
And it hurts like glass
My past
Cutting deep into my soul
Feeling so trapped by my own fears
I'm reaching out for a better today

Trying to find a better way
Something I feel I don't deserve

I'm not focused on tomorrow
For it may never come
But I need a resolution
Of getting what I want

My mind is a pool of dreams
and nightmares
Reflection of a life
of misguided opportunity

What Lies Beneath

I find myself in a mental whirlwind
A storm of near hate
in a dark and dead place
Hair triggered disdain
for most those around me
How could I have found myself in such
an unhappy state?

Misery and pain were left
so far behind
And now they have found me
I feel like I'm running out of time
Near the brink of self-destruct

I pull myself out because I fear ruin
But the solutions continue to slip
though my reach
I have to help myself because others
cannot even begin
If I don't in this game of life,
I will never win

My heart is hurting
and my fingers bend
Tension is rippling through my skin

I scream out for help
but no one hears me

Why is there no concern?
They don't realize the pain I feel inside
My smile I wear as a veil
To cover up my sorrow
Oh God
I hope to make it through tomorrow
I hurt so much inside

My prayers take all of my energy
I can only hope that Jah hears me
Please help me pull out
find myself again
This cancerous pain is killing my
joyful soul
I want to reach out to others
Please, ya'll, don't you see?
It wouldn't be fair for them
to have to deal
This is what I feel
This is what I see
Why is it so hard being me?

I Feel

Sometimes I feel like I'm falling
into a hole
No one cares if I fade to black
I'm slowly fading away
And I don't know
if I will ever make it back
The other half of me
turns his back to the truth
Ignores my cries, my pain
and my desperation
Maybe he'll see it all when this half
jumps from the roof
How many times
do I have to shout and scream
To a room of plugged ears
No one hears me
No one cares... if I disappear
Which I already have
I'm just marching through my life
Until it's either done or repaired
I almost don't care
I probably wouldn't even fit in there
Sometimes I feel like
I'm falling into a hole
No one cares if I fade to black

I'm scared, getting frustrated
and at the end of my rope
I really don't think much longer
can I cope
I used to be happy; used to feel free
Now I feel like a slave
Not allowed to be me
Maybe this me is not so good after all

I wonder if anyone would really miss
me

Zero Gravity

When you reach this high
There is no coming down
The way it feels
Love heals
You can't touch the ground
The way love winds your curvy roads
Until there is no ... feeling
Uplifting like a hit of espresso
You don't hear me though
When you reach this high
There is no coming down
Full of desire
I wanna go higher
Another twilight
You got my zone going crazy
No loving like you and me baby
I feel light
Like a vein I'm all tapped out
No air, take me there
To the peaks of mountainous synergy
Divided greatly by lustful energy

Take me there

Of a Child

Wherever is the life of a child?
The abundant innocence and silly
antics of youth
Without a care in the world
Laughter and stomach ripping
chuckles
When a glance or brow raising
mischief of another
Was like a secret code of jesting
No reason
No point
Just the life of a child
Full of innocence and silly antics
of youth
Why is there a crime in a grownup
wanting to recapture it?
The time when we didn't grow up
too fast
A child's heart is light, it is pure
Who doesn't wish to recapture their
youth, if just for a moment?
Go back where the wild things roamed
Setting up forts and teepees
in our homes
Who doesn't wish that?

We all do
But in our world
A world of what is to be right and what
is looked upon as wrong
It's almost a crime
to sing a child's song
The judging eyes wonder when such a
man reaches for recaptured youth
Has anyone stopped to think?
The stories that brought much magic
and wonderment to our childhoods
Were created by men who went back
to their youth
To share a colorful world with children
and parents alike
It was these men who relived their
childhood
Who through the imagination of
children, created theme parks and
never lands and taught us to engage in
the wild rumpus and roar of life
Those moments remain in the hearts
of all of us until the grave
Those are what our greatest childhood
memories are made
There is a still a child in each of us
I'm grateful for that little girl

May she never leave my soul
To me those memories are worth more
than a pot of gold

She Speaks

The moon is full
Like a guide on the hollow
Alone in the pasture
She wanders wondering
Heart full of pain
More loss than gain
She speaks
To that burning moon
On a summer night
'I give you all of my might'
Legs weaken
She speaks
Lips numb, can't spit a sound
Hands thrown to the Heavens
Pleading
Begging
Her body speaks movement
'Can you hear me?' she asks
A soft breeze grazes her flesh
Inner calm, like a peaceful psalm
Is what she longed for
She speaks
Without a word
She speaks
To that burning moon

She speaks...

To creation

Wanderlust of My Mind

Wandering
Thoughts are like waves crashing
against mounds of sand
Embracing
Metaphoric oceans that I long for
Curiosity of my heart continuing
I want to get there
Gives me life
Thoughts and ideals
Tidal waves and hills
It's perfectly dangerous
Fear of drowning
The struggle is worth the journey back
to perfection
Strong arms holding me
Taking me in passionate embraces
He doesn't mean it
My body asks why
Wandering
Embracing
Wishing and Hoping
Is it a cover for happiness?
Lusting to belong somewhere
Someplace other than here

Within myself
Is the hollow and darkness
Emotional geography is breaking
down
Confusion is constant
and I need a rescuer
Hurry before the next level begins
Wandering
Embracing
Trying to deface me
One day, the fear will be gone
Then, I will be free

Don't Call Me Barstow
(Featured in the novel, The Hollywood Girl)

My heart always beat to a symphony
And danced to the tune of elegance
and Hollywood parties
Don't call me Barstow, I screamed
I never fit with the Regulars
Maybe I should have
My dreams were too lofty, they said
Perhaps they were right
No sooner than I was able to grasp
hold of the colorful fairytale
I longed for
It was smashed and
I nearly lost myself
Next time
I'll dream in black and white
That way at least, I can continue my
dance with Illusion
Reality, as it turned out, was too much
for me to handle

This is dedicated to You

The Poet Tree

Only darkness hears me
as I cling to my existence
The quarrel within
Waging against sin
Yet – I falter no more
Winning this war

We are as one soul
Synched hearts, without a sound
Emerging from agony

As I soar upward, escaping the night
The vision is clear
I must win this fight
Building my strength to carry your burden
Release your fear

Wonder sweeps over
The purpose is valid
I was pained to build my armor
To shield you from agony

My words are foliage
to heal your wounds
As did those of times past did me

Shielding each other

Like a poet tree

~
L. S.

www.ingramcontent.com/pod-product-compliance
Lightning Source LLC
Chambersburg PA
CBHW022124040426
42450CB00006B/845